C

IMAGE # 47

Mangia Bene

Casale Family Recipes & Memories from Our House to Yours

by James L. Casale

TABLE OF CONTENTS

PROLOGUE

This is the second edition of my family cook book. I did not intend to write a second edition. A dear friend, Diane Nardone Cook, after trying out the meatball recipe and loving the results, called and asked to buy five more copies. I did not have any more copies.

My first publisher required that I purchase at least 100 copies at a time. The cost was exorbitant. Even though I sold the first 100 copies in a few weeks, I didn't intend to purchase another 100 copies. Therefore, I decided to self-publish a second version, add 30 more recipes, and a lot more pictures, and make it available on amazon where one, two, or 10 copies can be ordered by anyone without going through me. I hope you enjoy this version. It's a great gift for any occasion. It fits in a Christmas stocking. will also make a great gift.

It is available at amazon.com, on Amazon.com

DEDICATION

TO MY PARENTS FRANK VICTOR CASALE AND CARMELINA CATHERINE PUMA CASALE

By James L. Casale

My parents were my heroes. Any success I have enjoyed on this planet is attributable to their unconditional love, guidance, hard work, and sacrifices. They were both first generation Italian Americans who loved their culture, their Catholic faith and Italian food. They always provided me, my brother, my sisters, relatives, friends, and often the neighborhood with wholesome and nutritious meals.

My siblings and I love to eat, cook, and entertain. The life lessons and cooking lessons provided to us by our parents are their legacy to us, their grandchildren, and their great grandchildren. The purpose of this book is to keep their memory alive in the hearts and souls of all their loved ones and anyone interested in extraordinarily simple and delicious Italian specialties.

In 1995, my parents celebrated their 50th wedding anniversary.

TO MY BIG BROTHER JOSEPH VINCENT CASALE (1935-2016)

I also dedicate this cookbook to my big brother, Joe. He was a loving, generous, and loyal son, brother, husband, father, uncle, cousin, grandfather, and friend. I was blessed with the best big brother ever. I looked up to him and wanted to be like him. He loved everything Italian; the food, wine, traditions, and the entire culture. He was a proud United States Marine and a personal friend of Frank Sinatra who tried to hire Joe as a bodyguard in the mid-sixties.

I could fill many pages about his exploits, his adventures, and his largesse. He was always fun to be around and always took care of his little brother. Everybody who met him has a Joe Casale story. I miss him terribly. I love you bro. God Bless you.

My big brother took me to Italy and Sicily in 1991 to celebrate my 50th birthday.

APPRECIATION

I extend my heartfelt thanks and appreciation to my brother Joe, sisters, Stephanie and Francesca for not only contributing to this book but also for their loving support that helped me keep the memory of our parents alive. My daughter Karen, my son James and my niece Debbie also contributed to this special family book and I thank them for their contributions. And a special thank you to my wife, Janet, for her patience and her contributions.

PART ONE

Memories

By James L. Casale

MOM

While my father has been crowned by his family and friends as the King of Tomato Sauce and the originator of most of the important recipes in this book, it must be noted that my mother was also a terrific cook. She pre-dated Rachel Ray and could put a delicious, quick and substantive meal on the table in less than 30 minutes. And, she exceeded all expectations, because she did this after a full day's work.

Actually, my interest in cooking began when I attempted to help my mother as she prepared an evening meal after an arduous day at the dress factory. My motivation to help was twofold: 1) mom was exhausted and I felt sorry for her, and 2) I was hungry.

My mother's workday began at 6:30 AM when she boarded the New Haven Railroad commuter train at the Harrison, NY train station. It whisked her into Manhattan in about 45 minutes. Her day ended at 6:30 PM when the train delivered her back to Harrison. She worked very hard as a dressmaker. Her work was piece work, i.e., she was paid by the number of garments she finished. She was always one of the top producers at the factory. She trudged home every night carrying the usual array of cake and cookies she purchased at Grand Central Station while waiting for her train to depart. More reliable than a mail carrier, she did this in all kinds of weather. I never remember her taking a sick day.

This line of work may be the reason Carmelina Catherine Puma Casale did not share my father's passion for cooking and entertaining. She was too damned tired o do much other than rest, say the rosary, and attack her beloved crossword puzzles. But she always made time to watch *Wheel of Fortune* and *Jeopardy.*

She was always gracious when people were in our house, but she preferred her quiet time. She is quietly resting in Heaven as you read this. She's my hero, always was; always will be.

INSERT IMAGE # 17

DAD

Due to my father's line of work as an insurance investigator, he had more time on his hands to cook and prepare meals. If he were home, he cooked the evening meal or sometimes would prepare it in advance so my mother would not have to cook. His passions were cooking, entertaining and Big Band music.

My father's nickname was *Reddy.* He was a red headed Sicilian. His father was born in a small town in the hills of Sicily, Villa Rosa. In his younger days in the 1930s, he started a band and named it the *Santa Fe Jazz Ramblers.* He played drums and the band played in some local clubs in New York City. He took a stage name that paid tribute to his idol, *Rudolph Valentino* .Hence, he became Reddy Valentino.

During the 70s, he resurrected his passion for Big Band music and created the Reddy Valentino Orchestra. They played local gigs and are still going strong today under the guidance of Scott Wenzel. Scott kept the name and the band continues to play engagements in Westchester County, NY.

I attended a concert during the summer of 2015. The band played to an enthusiastic crowd in a section of Playland Park in Rye, NY. One of the sax players was a former student of mine when I was the Principal of Preston School in West Harrison.

My father joined the Navy in 1943 during World War II and was sent to the Philippines. He never told me how it happened, but he was in charge of the officers' eating establishment. He named it Reddy's Sky Bar

Dad was a gifted host who –at different times-owned and operated two very different restaurants. The first restaurant, *Casale's*, was opened in 1960 in Mamaroneck on the Post Road. When he bought it, it was a non-descript neighborhood beer joint where locals went for a shot and a beer. I was his underage bartender. In less than six months, three deep at the bar was not unusual and the dining room was bursting with people gorging themselves on great Italian food. He was not the chef. He was the host; he loved people too much and they loved him.

His second venture as a restaurateur occurred in 1965 in Rye N.Y. near Oakland Beach. He converted an ice cream shack into a casual steak house which he named the *Cove East*. This was a real test of my dad's popularity because this place was way off the proverbial "beaten path." Again, within six months he was doing a booming business.

I learned a lot from him about the restaurant business. He was a natural. He was not the chef in either restaurant. Dad was the charismatic host with a thousand friends. People loved to be around him. He had the gift of gab and a million stories.

Occasionally, he did prepare some of his favorite, but simple dishes such as his delicious pasta fagioli, and offer it to the bar patrons for free. As I said, he had a gift, and the customers kept returning. His largesse also extended to all dinner patrons. He always sent over a free after dinner drink to every customer. It tasted like Galliano, but didn't cost as much. It was called Sicilian Gold.

My father's version of *his* style of Sicilian cooking could be labeled as *simple* or *peasant* food. It was prepared without a long list of **never** measured ingredients. I don't know where or from whom he learned to cook. I never asked him; he never told me. Regardless, his meals were dominated by pasta and his unmatched sauce. He also cooked delicious bean and vegetable dishes –of course- with pasta.

He spoiled me so much that the only meals I can order in an Italian restaurant are pizza, fish, and veal dishes. The only exception I make is the Pasta Puttanesca at Sofia's Restaurant in Harrison, NY. As the familiar expression goes, "It's to die for." No, my dad never made it, but I did include my favorite recipe for it in this book. I tried it in other restaurants, but Sofia's and Maria, who prepared it, set he standard for me and I never enjoyed it again until I made my own.

Thanks Mom and Dad
By
Francesca Casale D'Angelo

My parents, Frank and Carmel Casale, were the best cooks on the planet. They didn't make fancy dishes or extravagant desserts, but what they did make was always delicious and everybody wanted some. I'll never forget the look on our guests' faces if they were invited to our standard Sunday dinner that started promptly at 2:00 pm. They would all fill up on several plates of macaroni with tons of "sauce" and meatballs (my father's masterpiece), followed by a salad.

Then, to their surprise, came more food; the roasted chicken parts and potatoes in all their glory seasoned to perfection. You just couldn't resist eating a little bit more. The dessert was coffee usually served with fruit (the mere smell of an orange reminds me of my dad), ice cream or sherbet, and, of course, my mother's favorite cookies, Vienna Fingers. Oh, I can't forget the green mint leaf candy either, mom loved it.

And, what about those fabulous meatballs? I put that recipe in my daughter Ashley's second grade class recipe book (almost 25 years ago) and people are still using it today claiming it is the best of all time....naturally.

If I close my eyes and think back on those wonderful days of eating the best food in town, I can't help but still smell my mom's chicken soup which really did *cure the common cold and feed the soul*. When I make my father's pasta and peas, my family eats it for breakfast, lunch and dinner.

Ah, back to the sauce that was simmering all morning until it drove you crazy. It was like going to heaven just to dip your bread in the sauce, and the drippings in the frying pan where the meatballs were fried. Probably, our Sunday dinner was one of the main reasons just to go to church, because when you came home it was almost time to eat! Crumb buns from the local bakery can only cure your appetite for so long. Dad just loved his crumb buns and dipped them relentlessly in his coffee, in addition to every other donut and piece of cake.

Oh, and one more thing. I can't forget dad's Chicken Marsala. It has become a staple on my dinner menu. I make it from memory and, like my dad, I am not sure of any of the measurements. My brother Jimmy did put the recipe in this book.

Truly, there is nothing like being Italian and eating like one. Family *and* good food is a match made in heaven. Thanks Mom and Dad for not only feeding me with such delicious food, but more importantly, filling my heart and soul with the riches of your wisdom and love.

INSERT IMAGE # 4

Sunday Dinner

By

Joe Casale

As I recall, Sunday dinner was at 2:00 PM exactly. First came the pasta, then after a brief respite, salad was served. All the dishes were cleared and while many sat in the living room, the table was re-set and the "meat" course, whatever it happened to be that day, was brought out. After that, the table was again cleared, and coffee, cake, and the ever present Jell-O were put on the table. Once again, those who did not help, got off their butts in the living room, and came to the table. Sunday dinner usually lasted about three hours. Because there was always plenty of food, Ray Donovan, the police chief's son and our neighbor, once he had tasted Mom and Dad's cooking, always managed to convince *his* mother that he was not hungry, and showed up sometime on Sunday afternoon, to eat whatever he could. This usually carried over into Monday, when I would take a meatball sandwich to school, and Dad's reputation having spread, I was bombarded with requests for a "bite". Plain and simple, nobody cooked like Mom and Dad.

INSERT IMAGE #3

My father was in the Navy during WWII prompting my brother Joe to wear a sailor uniform. Joe later became a captain in the United States Marine Corps.

Friday Night Specials
By
James L. Casale

Dad's dislike for fish and the *no meat rule* on Fridays were the source for the section titled, *Friday Night Specials*. Our Friday night meals consisted of the following: pasta fagioli, pasta and peas, pasta and squash, pasta and lentils, escarole and beans and pastina (tiny pasta and butter). These meals-basically peasant food-were satisfying, wholesome, nutritious and easy to prepare. Italian bread was a staple at our table and enjoyed by soaking it into the juices of these savory dishes.

IMAGE # 2

Mom's Artichokes
By
Stephanie Casale Carnavalla

Mom made the best stuffed artichokes. She served them at all of our holiday Dinners: Easter, Thanksgiving, and Christmas. There were never enough, because they were so popular. She never measured the ingredients but I was determined to write everything down and create a recipe which is shared in this book. As hard as I try, my artichokes are never as good as my mother's. However, my children and siblings tell me that I am getting close to mom's perfect recipe.

INSERT IMAGE # 5
Stephanie and Jimmy in front of their stoop at 109 East 127th Street.

Grandma's Faux Communion Bread
By
Debbie Carnavalla Nye (grandchild)

When I was in elementary school, my mother had a habit of leaving me and my brothers, Steve and Dee, with Grandma Casale because my mom needed a break from us and our shenanigans. I don't think my mom realized what a treat it was to be dropped off at Gram's house.

Gram lived in a two story house in Harrison, NY. Like all good Italian Americans my grandparents had a kitchen in the basement. This arrangement, of course, was in addition to the regular kitchen on the first floor. The always damp basement and kitchen was *the* place to be. The décor was unusual. Mexican men in sombreros were painted on the walls-courtesy of grandpa's cousin, Pat Stigliani.

The floors were littered with Gram's fabric, she was an expert seamstress, the old Singer sewing machine was front and center, and the second hand couches welcomed jumping and eating and playing; they never complained. Neither did Gram.

When I was about eight years old, my obsession for bland tasteless food was manifested in Gram's communion bread. Her tools: rolling pins, pans, hand mixers and the ingredients: flour, water and salt were all *mine*. While I was playing Chef Debbie, my brothers were painting with ketchup, mustard and mayo on paper, *and* the walls. "Let them play", Gram would exclaim, "It's good for them." Gram was the best and is sorely missed.

INSERT IMAGE#30
Amanda, Sarah and baby Holly

Unfortunately, I Grew Up in Florida
By
Karen Casale Masliah (The king's granddaughter)

My family moved to Naples, Florida in 1969. Except for a brief time in the late 70s when my grandparents moved to Florida, my brother James and I weren't fortunate enough to sample their memorable cooking and infinite generosity. Fortunately, when my father became principal of Purchase School in 1984, we moved back to Harrison, New York, and my real memories of my grandparents cooking began. I was 16 years old.

I remember being so obsessed with my grandpa's minestrone soup, I made him write down every ingredient. Then, I went to Daitch Shopwell, purchased all the ingredients, brought them to grandpa's house, and watched the master make it. I make it a few times every winter. My family and friends love it. I, like my grandparents, don't measure anything when I cook. It's a gift I inherited from them (along with the Casale/Puma sugar addiction).

I also remember grandma's "green salad". I don't ever remember her making a different salad. It consisted of iceberg lettuce fresh chopped garlic, fresh chopped onion, and the dressing was olive oil, white distilled vinegar and salt and pepper. That's it. And let me tell you, my 21 year old daughter, to this day, asks me for grandma Casale's salad. We love it, but now we have brought it to the new millennium by using romaine, or arugula, or even baby kale. But the dressing always remains the same. Don't knock fresh chopped garlic in your salad until you have tried it, Trust me.

I used to love hanging out at my grandparent's house. It wasn't just because I loved them, by the way they both had a great sense of humor, it was also because you could be sure there would be Neapolitan ice cream in the freezer as well as Vienna fingers in the pantry. Yahoo!

I loved going to the Harrison Bake Shop and buying French crullers for grandpa and sfogliatelles for grandma. I think about them often and miss just being able to pop over and sit at the kitchen table to chat.

Grandpa and grandma would be so proud to see their family recipes in print. May their memories live on as we prepare these wonderful dishes for our families and hopefully the future generations of Casales, Pumas, our relatives, and, friends.

INSERT IMAGE # 56

Karen and Olivia (Are they sisters?)

Grandpa and the Sauce
By
James Francis Casale (The King's grandson)

Growing up in Florida, I didn't get to spend as much time with my Grandpa and Grandma as I would have liked. I do have very fond memories of family visits to New York, and spending time with my grandparents, and of course enjoying the delicious meals they prepared for us.

During visits, I remember tagging along with my Grandpa during – let's call it – pre-sauce preparation. We drove off in his baby blue Chevy (my Grandpa loved the color blue) on a 'pilgrimage' to purchase all the ingredients needed for The Sauce and the Sunday meal. The first stop was Food City in Harrison where we bought the canned tomatoes and paste. "Grandpa, buy these tomatoes, Hunts." 'No Rabbit, grab those other ones and put them in the cart, they're on sale." I learned that you can buy the right items for the sauce and still be thrifty.

We weren't done. We returned to the car and drove to the next stop, M&M Market. "Grandpa, can I turn the radio on?" "No Rabbit, it wears down the battery." Instead my Grandpa would whistle a song for me; he was a great whistler. At M&M Market, we bought the spices needs for the sauce and produce for the salad. My Grandpa showed me how to pick the basil. The leaves must be very green (no brown spots) and the stems have to look fresh too. We also bought fresh parsley.

We weren't done yet. Next stop was John the Butcher. John was Grandpa's man for fresh ground round. It made the best meatballs. While you could buy the on-sale tomatoes at Food City, I learned you don't get thrifty when it comes to the meat for the meatballs.

We might have made a final stop at Westchester Bakery for a loaf of fresh, crusty Italian bread. They didn't make bread like that in Florida.

Page 14

didn't learn how to actually make the Sauce until years later (my Dad taught me). The tradition of the Sauce, however, began for me with those simple but very special trips with my Grandpa.

MEATBALL MEMORIES
By
James L Casale

Along with the title of King of Sauce, my dad was also the best maker of meatballs. Most meatball makers think their meatballs are the best; they're not. My father kept it simple and I have tried to follow his example. One did not chew on my father's meatballs; they seemed to melt in your mouth.

I have politely eaten other people's homemade meatballs and watched the celebrity chefs on TV make their version. There is no comparison. Dad always used "fresh" ingredients; he always bought ground round from John the Butcher on Halstead Avenue in Harrison. I do not ever remember seeing packaged meat from the supermarket in our house as long as John was in business.

My only variation from my father's recipe is that I use ground sirloin and organic ingredients when I can find them. I usually grow my own parsley and basil. He did not measure anything and neither do I, but for this book I will include measurements with the following caveat: Sauce and meatballs are prepared to an individual's taste buds. Some like more garlic than others, or more cheese. You will have to practice until you get it your way.

In the 1930s my father formed a jazz band called the Santa Fe Jazz Ramblers. He was the drummer. He took the stage name of Reddy Valentino. He had red hair and his idol was Rudolph Valentino.

RED GOLD

BY

James L. Casale

If oil is *black gold* then my father's sauce is Red Gold. Everybody who had the opportunity to taste his sauce marveled about its exceptionality. Comments from friends, relatives and strangers such as," this is better than my mother's sauce" were common. When I made it for my roommate in college, Joe Costella, whose parents owned an Italian restaurant on Long Island; he joined the throng of worshipers.

My father did not buy a specific brand of tomatoes; he bought whatever was on sale. He was the quintessential coupon cutter. He usually bought whole tomatoes and blended them in the blender. I did that for years until I discovered how time saving it was to purchase crushed tomatoes, and I liked the consistency. However, I am told and have read that whole tomatoes are better than other varieties.

There seems to be some consensus among food experts that the pricey San Marzano canned tomatoes are the premium choice among the many available brands. I have tried this expensive brand and admit that they are very good. The King of Sauce bought mainly the brand that was on sale. Usually, it was the Red Pack brand, but he made a "killer" sauce from any brand.

I usually buy the Contadina brand from Costco. This 105 ounce can of crushed tomatoes is a bargain. If there were a Costco in our neighborhood when my father was weaving his magic, I know he would have stocked the pantry with it; probably a six month supply.

Part of the secret to this successful recipe is not *in* the recipe: Dad loved to cook and entertain and he did so with affection, love, joy and gusto.

"Never eat more than you can lift"
Miss Piggy (created 1976 by Jim Henson and Frank Oz)

HELPFUL HINTS
"Cook because you love it"

- Use only fresh ingredients; organics are best.
- Buy your meat from a butcher (the best supermarkets have butchers). Buy meat and poultry that is not processed and is free of anti-biotics and growth hormones
- Cook pasta "al dente" toward hardness. Mushy pasta is a sign that labels you as a lousy cook. Add several tablespoons of salt to the boiling water **before** you put in the pasta.
- Basic staples: all kinds of pasta, fresh herbs (basil, parsley, oregano; grow your own if you can), extra virgin cold pressed olive oil, red pepper flakes(pepperoncini)ricotta, (spoon it over pasta for a blast of protein), mozzarella, ricotta salada (a great tasting soft grating cheese), parmigiana reggiano (recommended as a grating cheese), cannellini beans, and peas, chick peas, lentils.
- Do not let the pasta dry out after it is cooked. Add a cup of sauce and stir it into the pasta so it is coated and moist.
- If you don't like a thick sauce, add water to control the consistency. This takes several tries before you know what you are doing.
- You can spice almost anything with a few cherry peppers.
- **Note: Janet and I own many cookbooks authored by professional chefs and several loose-leaf books filed with recipes from magazines, newspapers and friends. Most recipes including those in this book are not perfect. It often takes several tries and some experimenting until you arrive at "your way". Think of these and other recipes as a framework for your own creative juices and cook with love and enthusiasm.**

I made this cutting board in shop class at Halstead Avenue School (renamed Parsons Memorial School). My mother used it regularly and now my daughter Karen uses it.

Part Two

The Sauce

"Everybody thinks their sauce is the best; but it ain't"
James L. Casale

"You can't die Grandpa, who's going to make the sauce?"

Francis Edward Casale, (the King's grandson)

THE SAUCE POEM

By
James L. Casale

We laughed out loud when this was said.
And now the King of Sauce is dead.
The King lives on in souls and hearts.
The recipe lives; we have all the parts.

Sauté fresh garlic, brown it never, in the finest olive oil.
Infuse with parsley, and stir with love; the aroma is worth the toil.
Now add tomatoes from the can, three cans will be just fine.
Salt and pepper to your taste; add fresh basil; never thyme.

Simmer low, cover on, for an hour plus or so.
Stir and watch, watch and stir, be prepared to nowhere go.

If marinara is not your choice, add your meat and sausage now.
The recipe for the king's meatballs, this poem will not allow.

By

James L. Casale

SAUCE vs GRAVY
By
James L. Casale

In my opinion, nothing in this book is as important as "THE SAUCE". The sauce is the centerpiece of many of your pasta, meat and fish dishes. For example: macaroni, spaghetti, lasagna, baked ziti, manicotti, ravioli, veal parmigiana, chicken parmigiana, chicken cacciatorre, eggplant parmigiana, and shrimp marinara will never be delicious if your sauce is not made correctly.

PLEASE DO NOT ALLOW ANYONE TO ENTER YOUR HOUSE WHO REFERS TO TOMATO SAUCE AS,"GRAVY". THESE PEOPLE ARE TO BE AVOIDED AT ALL COSTS.THEY ARE MISSING AT LEAST ONE GENE AND DON'T OWN A DICTIONARY.

GRAVIES ARE EXTRACTED FROM MEATS SUCH AS PORK, BEEF, CHICKEN, AND TURKEY. DO NOT ATTEMPT TO PURCHASE A BOTTLE OR CAN OF TOMATO GRAVY OR MARINARA GRAVY; THEY DO NOT EXIST. PLACING MEAT INTO YOUR TOMATO SAUCE DOES NOT MAKE IT GRAVY.

According to the Readers Digest Great Encyclopedia, the definition of gravy is as follows:

Gravy-The juice, melted fat, etc. exuded by cooked or cooking meat.

Insert image 57-
Cartoon by Laureen Grossman

The Sauce vs. Gravy Poem
By
James L. Casale

A young man named Davy longed to be in the Navy
And ply his trade as a cook
But Davy read never and ever and ever
And didn't own a book

When tested by the Navy on what's sauce or gravy
Young Davy was at a loss
He stumbled and mumbled and stuttered along
But knew not the difference between gravy and sauce

Needless to say, the young lad slipped away
And vowed to correct his mistake
He read several books and consulted with cooks
Now gravy he knows how to make

To drippings of beef or ham or lamb
Use flour, stir and add stock
Its color is brown, he now has it down
His knowledge is solid as a rock

And now for tomatoes but not potatoes
No longer will you be at a loss
Marry garlic and parsley to the finest olive oil
Add tomatoes, and now you have sauce

THE SAUCE RECIPE

BY

Frank V. Casale (The King of Sauce)

Commentary: If you have read diligently up to this point, it is clear that your sauce will define you, and your attempt to duplicate the recipes in this book. Take heart and don't be discouraged. It will take several or many attempts until you are satisfied. My father's original recipe included sautéing several beef bones and adding them to the sauce. He said the bones reduced the acidity in the tomatoes. Some people, like Clemenza in the *Godfather* movie, added sugar to the sauce to reduce acidity. Dad didn't and I never did.

Ingredients:

- 3 cans of crushed tomatoes – 33 oz. or 1 can Costco's Contadina Crushed Tomatoes(105oz.)
- 5-7 cloves of finely chopped garlic(more if you love garlic)
- ½ cup of freshly chopped parsley

- 3 tablespoons. extra virgin cold pressed olive oil (great buy at Costco)
- ½ cup fresh basil(torn into pieces)
- Salt & pepper to taste
- ½ cup of red wine(optional)
- ½ - ¾ cup of water; depends on the consistency of the tomatoes
- Crushed red pepper flakes(optional)
- Bay leaf(optional)
- Tomato paste (optional)

On low to medium heat, sauté the garlic in the olive oil and add the parsley. Stir with wooden spoon and enjoy the aroma for a few minutes. DO NOT BROWN the garlic. Add the tomatoes and stir thoroughly. Add the remainder of the ingredients except the basil and stir. If you decide to add the wine, wait until the sauce is simmering on a low boil. Simmer with cover on for first the hour; then uncovered for half an hour. Stir regularly. Add basil near the end of the cooking cycle. Experiment with the consistency you want.

If you are adding meatballs and sausage, brown them on all sides first, then add them at the beginning of the process so the sauce can absorb the meat flavors.

"You know you're Italian if you have enough cans of tomatoes in your house to last three years."

Mangia Bene

Part Three

Meat Recipes

IMAGE # 13

MEATBALLS

Commentary: Everybody who fancies himself or herself as a maker of meatballs thinks their meatballs are the best, but they "ain't." I will not order a restaurant's meatballs because they also do not measure up to the King's meatballs. Neither does the sauce. The standard comment from my grandkids who order meatballs in every restaurant is, "They are not as good as yours grandpa."

Ingredients:

- 1 lb. or 1$1/2$ lbs. of ground sirloin/or ground round
- Salt and pepper to taste*
- 4-6 cloves garlic(finely chopped)
- ½ cup of finely chopped fresh parsley
- ½ cup grated Italian cheese
- 1 egg
- ¼-1/2 cup water
- ½ cup to ¾ cup of unflavored breadcrumbs

Directions:

Start with a large bowl and gently press the meat down to resemble a large hamburger. Then salt and pepper it to your taste.

Add the remainder of the ingredients and mix by hand. I must confess here that I am seeking a specific texture when I am mixing the ingredients. If there is too much resistance in the mixture the meatballs will be hard. If the mixture is too soft the meatballs will not hold together when you fry them; practice and experiment.

Brown(do not cook through) the meatballs on all sides in a frying pan with light olive oil then place them gently in the sauce. My sister bakes or broils them.

Another friend microwaves them. I can't do it; my father won't let me. He's watching me.

MANGIA BENE

CHICKEN CASALE SICILIANA

Commentary: This savory dish was a favorite of the whole family. My father made it look so easy. The chicken fell off the bone and the flavors melded together to create a sumptuous dish.

Ingredients:

- One whole chicken cut into parts or just parts(removing the skin is optional)
- 4-5 medium potatoes; peeled and quartered
- 3-4 medium onions; quartered
- ½ cup olive oil
- 4-6 cloves of garlic; finely chopped
- 1 tbl. of oregano
- ¼ cup Italian parsley; finely chopped
- Salt and pepper to taste
- Peppers(optional); Cherry peppers make it spicy

Directions: In a mixing bowl combine the olive oil, garlic, parsley, and oregano. Coat each piece of chicken thoroughly in the olive oil mixture and place in a not too deep roasting pan. Leave space between pieces for the potatoes. Place the potatoes in the empty spaces around the chicken. Spread the onions on top of the chicken and potatoes. Salt and pepper the entire dish to your taste. Bake covered for 1 hour and 30 minutes at 350 degrees. Remove cover and bake for another 15-20 minutes.

INSERT IMAGE #46

MANGIA BENE

CHICKEN PICCATA

Commentary: This is easy. Most ingredients will be staples that you keep in your Italian kitchen. If you choose to buy the less expensive chicken breasts rather than the cutlets, slice them carefully and pound them to ¼ inch thickness. Actually, I ask the butcher to slice the breasts for me.

Ingredients:
- 4 boneless skinless chicken breasts
- All- purpose flour(organic)
- Salt and pepper
- 2-3 tablespoons of olive oil
- ¼ cup dry white wine
- 1 tablespoon minced garlic
- ½ cup organic chicken broth
- 1 tablespoon lemon juice(fresh)
- 1 tablespoon capers(drained)

- 2 tablespoons unsalted butter
- Lemon slices
- Fresh chopped parsley(garnish)

Directions:

Heat pan to medium high then add light olive oil. Season the cutlets on both sides with salt and freshly ground pepper. Dredge the cutlets in the flour (shake off excess flour), sauté on one side for 2-3 minutes then the other for 1-2 minutes. (must be cooked through). Transfer the cutlets to a warming platter.
Deglaze the pan with the wine, add the garlic. Cook until liquid is nearly evaporated. Add the broth, lemon juice and capers. Return the cutlets to the pan juices and cook for one more minute.

Veal Marsala

Commentary: I don't remember my father or mother making this dish, but it's basically the same as Chicken Marsala. I do remember that we enjoyed veal cutlets at least once a week. My parents fried them in olive oil and served them with a vegetable and a salad. John the Butcher (who else?), on Halstead Avenue was *the* place to get the best cutlets in town. This recipe has more ingredients than I prefer, but the results are worth it. Most ingredients should already be in your Italian pantry.

Ingredients: (serves four)
- 4- 6 cutlets pounded to about 1/4 inch
- Kosher salt
- Freshly ground pepper
- 3-4 tablespoons of unsalted butter
- 2-3 tablespoons of extra virgin olive oil

- 1 shallot finely chopped
- 2-3 large cloves of garlic finely chopped
- 2 teaspoons of fresh sage finely chopped
- All-purpose flour(organic if you can find it)
- 6-10 oz. of assorted mushrooms sliced thinly
- 2 Tbsp. capers rinsed and coarsely chopped
- ½ cup Marsala wine
- 1 teaspoon lemon juice
- 1/4-1/2 cup of organic chicken broth
- 2 tablespoons parsley finely chopped

Directions:

Salt and pepper each side of the cutlets, dredge in flour (shake off excess flour)
In a large frying pan on medium to high heat add 1 tablespoon of olive oil and 1 tablespoon of butter. Saute' the cutlets for about a minute on each side until golden brown, remove from pan and set aside in a warming plate. (You may have to do this in batches)

In the same pan, add another tablespoon of olive oil and butter and sauté the garlic, capers and shallots for 30-45 seconds.
Add the mushrooms and sauté until tender (2-3 minutes).
Add the wine and simmer until reduced by half.

If you like the consistency of this tasty and fragrant gravy-I like it thick-don't add much broth. If you think it's too thin, simmer it until it reduces.
Return the cutlets to your gravy, a few at a time, and heat through.
Place the cutlets on individual dinner plates, spoon the gravy over the veal and serve

NOTE: FOR CHICKEN OR PORK MARSALA, FOLLOW THE SAME RECIPE.

MANGIA BENE

BRACIOLA

Commentary: My mother and father took turns making this from scratch, and they were always excellent. Remember to get your meat from a butcher, but if you are feeling lazy or just pressed for time, the butcher at the Italian specialty store will pound the meat for you, or prepare the complete braciola for you.

Ingredients:

- 2-4 small flank steaks
- Parsley
- 4-5 cloves of garlic; finely chopped
- Salt and pepper
- 3 T. of olive oil

Directions: Pound the flank steaks to a ¼ inch thickness. Lay flat and sprinkle with parsley, fresh garlic and salt and pepper. Roll up into a small log and tie both ends with string. Brown all sides in olive oil then place in "The Sauce". They will be tender in about an hour.

Note: You can also make pork braciola. Use pork tenderloin.

MANGIA BENE

CHICKEN CACCIATORE

Commentary: My father didn't make this too often, but when he did, it was delicious. This is my wife Janet's recipe and it is equally sumptuous.

Ingredients:
- 1/4-1/2 cup olive oil
- 10-12 pieces of chicken-skin optional
- ½ lb. mushrooms
- 2 large onions; sliced
- 3-5 cloves garlic; chopped (more for garlic lovers)
- 2 large bell peppers; sliced lengthwise(remove core and seeds)
- 1 lb.-1lb.1/2 chopped or diced tomatoes
- ¼ cup red wine
- 1 teaspoon sea salt
- 1 teaspoon pepper
- 1 teaspoon red pepper flakes
- 1 teaspoon oregano
- 5-6 leaves chopped basil
- 1lb. spaghetti

Directions:

Heat frying pan first on medium/medium high, then add half the olive oil. Brown chicken on all sides; remove from pan. Add onion and cook till tender; add garlic to the onions but do not brown it. Remove from pan. Sauté mushrooms until brown. Add tomatoes to the mushrooms and stir, then add chicken, onions, garlic, peppers, salt, pepper, red pepper flakes, and oregano. Stir again and cook on low boil, covered, for 45 minutes. Blend in wine and basil and continue to cook uncovered for 20 minutes. Ladle the mixture over the cooked (al dente) spaghetti. Note: If you do not own a large, deep and heavy skillet, use what you have for frying and sautéing, and then place all ingredients in a large heavy pot.

CHICKEN PARMIGIANA

Commentary: Without a doubt, this was one my father's favorite dishes to eat. I cannot remember when he didn't order this in a restaurant. Of course, when your sauce is a good as his, you will love it more than you do now.

Ingredients:

- 1-1/2 lbs. chicken cutlets
- 2 eggs (whisked together)
- 2 c. breadcrumbs
- ½ c. olive oil (I use light olive oil for frying)
- ½ - 1lb. shredded mozzarella cheese
- "The Sauce"

Directions:

Follow the directions for veal parmigiana.

ITALIAN MEATLOAF/ ITALIAN HAMBURGERS

Commentary: Meatloaf can be boring, but visualize eating a meatball dripping with the king's marinara sauce: Boredom is now over. Add mozzarella to the middle of the loaf for extra flavor, moisture, and more protein.

Ingredients:

- 1 lb. ground sirloin or ground round
- Same as meatballs(see recipe)
- 1/2cup chopped onions
- ½ cup chopped green pepper

Directions:

Follow meatball directions. Place ingredients in a meatloaf baking pan and bake in oven at 350 degrees for 45 minutes to 1 hour.

Note: The cheese, breadcrumbs and water help determine the consistency. Also, if you like it spicy, add your favorite hot sauce or cherry peppers.

MANGIA BENE

STEAK PIZZAIOLI

Commentary: There was no filet mignon in my house when I was growing up. But when my father made this, it was heavenly. Chuck steak or chuck roast are inexpensive cuts of meat that can be made flavorful with this recipe. You can substitute other cuts of meat. Try it in a crock pot.

Ingredients:

- 1 large inexpensive cut of chuck steak
- 1 can(33 oz.) of crushed, diced or hand crushed whole tomatoes
- 2 medium onions; sliced
- 2-4 cloves of garlic; sliced
- ½ teaspoon oregano
- Salt and pepper to taste

Directions:

Sear the steak on the grill or under the broiler, and then place the steak in a baking pan. Salt and pepper it. Smother the steak with the tomatoes, onions and garlic and sprinkle on the oregano. Bake, covered, in a 350 degree oven for 1 -2 hours. Or use your crock pot.

VEAL PARMIGIANA

Commentary: We enjoyed fried veal cutlets at least once a week without the cheese or the sauce. My mom or dad just fried them in olive oil and served them with a vegetable and maybe a potato. I should have eaten more veggies and less candy, cake, ice cream, and soda; maybe I would have grown to six feet tall.

Ingredients:

- 1 lb. of veal cutlets
- 2 eggs (whisked)
- 2 c. breadcrumbs
- ½ c. olive oil
- ½ -1 lb. shredded mozzarella cheese
- "The Sauce"

Directions:

Dip each cutlet first into the egg mixture and then coat both sides with the breadcrumbs. Fry the cutlets in light olive oil until done. Pat each cutlet with paper towel to remove some of the oil and set aside. Cover the bottom of an appropriate sized backing dish with sauce. Create layers of cutlets with sauce and mozzarella between each layer. Top off with a layer of mozzarella. Bake in oven at 325 for 20-30 minutes.

MANGIA BENE

Part Four

Friday Night Specials

INSERT IMAGE #10

FRESH TOMATOES-YELLOW SQUASH AND FARFALLE

Commentary: This is a very popular dish that I usually make in the warm summer months with the fresh and ripe tomatoes from my garden. It's very easy to prepare and always delicious.

Ingredients: **(serves four)**

- 6-8 fresh very juicy garden tomatoes
- 4-6 garlic cloves; finely chopped
- ¼-1/2 c. basil leaves; chopped
- 2-3 medium yellow squash; do not peel
- Salt and pepper
- 2 tablespoons olive oil
- 1 lb. butterfly pasta(farfalle)
- Grated cheese

Directions: Slice tomatoes into quartered slices (reserve all juice; the juice is the key) and place in large bowl. Tomatoes must be room temperature. Add the garlic and basil to the tomatoes and stir gently. Slice the squash lengthwise then into small bite sized pieces. Wash but do not peel the squash. Saute' the squash in the light olive oil until soft (5-7 minutes). Add the squash to the tomato mixture, add salt and pepper, mix gently and leave at room temperature. While the squash, tomatoes, garlic and basil are meeting, greeting and getting to know each other, boil the water and cook the pasta al dente. When the pasta is done, drain immediately, place in individual serving dishes and spoon the tomato and squash mixture over the pasta. If desired, sprinkle your favorite grated cheese on top.

MANGIA BENE

PASTA and ZUCCHINI

Commentary: I love this recipe, but I love the way my sister Stephanie makes it; it's soupy. I put both recipes in this section. As always, try them out and add your own unique ingredients and techniques. If you love zucchini with an accompaniment of sauce, you will love either version. My mother usually made this with spaghetti broken up into small pieces.

Ingredients: (serves four)
- 2-3 cloves of garlic finely chopped
- 1 medium onion sliced thinly
- 1 can of tomato sauce (33 oz.)
- Salt and pepper to taste
- Red pepper flakes(optional)
- 2-3 medium sized zucchini
- 3 tablespoons of olive oil
- ½ -1 cup of water
- 2-3 oz. of elbow macaroni or per person

Directions:
Sauté' the onions in the olive oil until translucent. Add the garlic to the onions and sauté for a few minutes; do not brown. Add the sauce and the water. Add salt and pepper to taste.-Add the peeled and thinly sliced zucchini to the sauce.-Simmer 30-40 minutes or until the zucchini is tender.- Cook the elbows or the broken up spaghetti al dente.-Ladle the zucchini mixture over the pasta in individual serving dishes.

Note: You can substitute yellow squash for zucchini; it has a shorter cooking time than zucchini.

MANGIA BENE

PASTA AND ZUCCHINI #2

COMMENTARY: This is my sister Stephanie's recipe. It's soupier than mine so try both and adjust it to your own taste buds.

Ingredients: (serves four)

- 1 small can (8 oz.)of tomato sauce
- 1 small onion; chopped
- 3-4 cloves of garlic; chopped
- 3-4 zucchini; peeled and quartered
- 2-3 tablespoons olive oil
- Dash of oregano
- 1 lb. of ditalini or elbow pasta
- Salt and pepper to taste
- Crushed red pepper flakes(optional)
- Cold water -1-2 cups as desired

Directions:

Sauté the onion for 3-5 minutes until it's translucent. Add the garlic to the sautéing onions; do not brown. Add the tomato sauce and the cold water. When it comes to a boil, lower the heat and simmer ten minutes. Add the zucchini and the salt and pepper. Boil the pasta to al dente. Drain the pasta;

ladle into individual serving dishes and then add the soupy sauce. (DO NOT MIX ALL THE PASTA WITH ALL THE SAUCE. THE PASTA WILL ABSORB THE LIQUID AND IT WILL BE TOO THICK)

INSERT IMAGE # 52

AGLIO E OGLIO
(garlic and oil)

Commentary: This is a classic recipe found in most Italian restaurants. If you love garlic and pasta(who doesn't?), learn this easy recipe quickly because you can-at any time- jazz it up by adding clams, shrimp, lobster, or crab meat.

Ingredients: (serves four)

- 5-8 large garlic cloves- sliced or chopped
- ½ cup fresh parsley-chopped fine(no stems)
- 2 anchovy filets
- 3-4 tablespoons olive oil
- ¾ lb. of linguini or spaghetti
- Grated cheese(optional)
- Red pepper flakes(optional)
- Salt and pepper

Directions:

Over low heat, sauté the anchovies until they liquefy. The anchovies will melt and delicately flavor this mixture. Add the garlic and parsley and gently sauté for a few minutes and then set aside. (DO NOT BROWN THE

GARLIC UNLESS YOU WANT TO; I DON'T BUT SOME RESTAURANTS DO. Boil the pasta in salted water and cook until al-dente; save 2 ladles of the pasta water. Drain the pasta, add the pasta to the garlic mixture and add some of the pasta water to the mixture and mix all together. If you do not add water the dish will be too dry. Add enough water to get the consistency you want, but don't make it soupy. Serve in individual dishes and top with grated cheese, red pepper flakes, and salt and pepper.

MANGIA BENE

PASTA FAGIOLI
(pasta and cannellini beans)

Commentary: Ignore people who refer to this dish as "pasta fazool". Fazool is not in the Italian dictionary and does not exist in the beautiful Italian language. It is, unfortunately, found in a few Italian songs sung by Louie Prima and Dean Martin. No offense to them; I love them both and the songs rhyme better with *fazool* than *fagioli*.
I enjoy this meal more than the finest steak. I grew up with it and both my mother and father made this with their Sicilian love for simple, but delicious and nutritious food. My parents did not use broth; they used water and it was still delicious.

Ingredients: (serves four)
- -2 cans cannellini beans
- -2 or 3 cloves of garlic; finely chopped

- -1 medium onion; chopped or thinly sliced
- -1 celery stalk; thinly sliced into small pieces
- -salt and pepper to taste
- -organic chicken or vegetable broth
- -1/2 pound of elbow macaroni or any other small pasta such as dittalini
- -2 to 4 tablespoons of olive oil

Directions:

Sauté the celery and onions in the olive oil until the onions are translucent; 3-5 minutes on medium. Add the garlic; do **NOT** brown. Drain and rinse the beans; (do **NOT** use the liquid in the cans) and add the beans to the sautéed ingredients. I stir the beans, the garlic, celery and onions before I cover the beans with broth. I think this helps coat the beans.

Now I cover the bean mixture with the broth. Add salt and pepper to taste; red pepper flakes are optional. Simmer 30 to 40 minutes.

Boil the pasta until al-dente; do NOT overcook the pasta; it should be chewy never mushy. Ladle bean mixture over pasta in individual serving dishes. Check the consistency you prefer. You may have to add more broth.

Notes:

1. Do **NOT** place the pasta in the same pot with the beans
2. Place the pasta in individual serving bowls then ladle in the bean mixture over each serving.
3. I never order this in restaurant because it's made ahead of time and the pasta is always mushy.
4. Many restaurants and individuals make this recipe with tomatoes or tomato sauce. The king did not and I do not use tomatoes.
5. If there are leftovers and you do not want to cook more pasta, feel free to mix the pasta and beans and heat up the next day for lunch or dinner.
6. All the ingredients in this recipe are Italian staples and should always be in your pantry or fridge.

7. If you like it with tomato sauce; try it. You are now the cook.

MANGIA BENE

PASTA LENTICCHIA
(Pasta and lentils)

Commentary: This is a very nutritious meal. Lentils contain iron and essential minerals. We all love it and continue to make it on a regular basis as a healthy break from meat products. I like mine soupy. Use elbow macaroni or any small pasta. My parents usually used spaghetti and broke it up into small pieces. We usually had several hundred boxes of spaghettini on hand. (Spaghettini is thin spaghetti, now it's called angel hair)

Ingredients:

- 2-3 cloves of garlic finely chopped (sound familiar?)
- 1 medium onion finely chopped
- 2 -3 tablespoons olive oil
- 1 celery stalk sliced thinly
- Organic vegetable broth or water; enough to cover the lentils. Add more broth later to maintain a soupy consistency.
- 1 finely chopped medium carrot
- Salt and pepper to taste
- Small chunks of cooked ham(optional)
- 2-3 oz. of elbows or spaghetti(broken into thirds) per serving

- 8 oz. of dry lentils or several cans of lentils(drain and rinse dry lentils and check for stones)

Directions:

- Sauté the onions and the celery in the olive oil until the onions are translucent; 3-4 minutes. Add the garlic- do not brown. Add the lentils and cover with broth or water; simmer until dry lentils are tender. I do not use canned lentils, but feel free to do so.

Note: When serving, ladle the mixture over the pasta in individual serving dishes; do not combine. Top with grated cheese if desired.

MANGIA BENE

PASTA PISELLI

(pasta and peas)

Commentary: I do not like peas, but I eat them with gusto in this dish. It was a Friday night staple; cheap, simple, easy to prepare and, it wasn't fish. This is one of the few tomato sauces in this book that include onions. When you master the simple and basic marinara sauce, everything you add to it tastes good.

Ingredients: (serves four)

- 3 tablespoons of olive oil
- 1 bag of frozen peas (I use organic peas)

- 2-4 cloves of garlic; finely chopped
- 1 medium onion; sliced thinly
- 1 can of tomato sauce; 33 ounces
- salt and pepper to taste
- -red pepper flakes to taste(optional)
- -elbow macaroni (2 -3ounces per person)

Directions:

Sauté the thinly sliced onions for 3-5 minutes in the olive oil. Add the garlic to the onions a few minutes before the onions are translucent. Add the sauce; salt and pepper and red pepper flakes (to taste).Add water to determine the consistency that you like. Simmer for 20 to 30 minutes. Boil the pasta and cook "al dente" (chewy); do not overcook.

Note: Ladle the mixture over the pasta in individual serving dishes; do not combine. A soupy mixture is best.

1. You can increase the flavor by adding fresh parsley to the onions and garlic while sautéing.
2. This dish can also be served with a dollop of ricotta for some added protein.
3. As with the pasta fagioli, I recommend that you do **NOT** add the pasta to the sauce mixture in the pot. Place the amount of pasta you want in each serving dish then add the sauce and peas.
4. If there are leftovers, then add the pasta to the sauce and have it for lunch the next day. If there is a lot of sauce left, freeze it for another time.

PASTA AND SHALLOTS

Commentary: This savory dish originated with my daughter Karen, a lover of all things Italian and a self- taught cook who will experiment with various combinations of ingredients. If you love shallots as much as we do, you will enjoy this simple meal.

Ingredients: (serves four)
- 3 tablespoons extra virgin olive oil
- 2 tablespoons butter
- 3 cloves garlic, finely chopped
- 10 shallots, thinly sliced
- Salt and pepper
- 1 lb. spaghetti
- ½ cup Italian parsley(flat leaf),chopped
- 1 cup parmigiana reggiano, grated

Directions:
Heat the olive oil and butter on low-medium in skillet. Add shallots, salt and pepper, and cook gently caramelizing the shallots (10-15 minutes). Add garlic next but do not brown. Boil water in large pot. Add 1 tablespoon of salt to the boiling water. Add spaghetti and cook al dente. When pasta is cooked, reserve a cup of the pasta water before draining and add to the shallots. Combine shallots, pasta, parsley, grated cheese, and more black pepper. Toss and serve.

MANGIA BENE

PASTA ALLA PUTANESCA

Commentary: My parents never made this dish. I discovered it at Sofia's Pizza Restaurant in Harrison, New York in the 90s. Sofia's served much more than pizza. The menu included a variety of Italian entrees exquisitely prepared by Maria, the owner's sister. It was so good, I had to stop and stare at it. I savored every bite. I vowed to learn how to make it. Here's my version.

Ingredients: (serves four)
- ½ cup olive oil
- ½ cup finely diced onion
- 3-5 garlic cloves, finely chopped
- 3 anchovy filets, chopped
- ¼ cup dry white wine
- 1 can (28/33 oz.) crushed tomatoes
- ¼ cup Gaeta or Kalamata olives, pitted & sliced
- 1 tablespoons capers, well drained
- Salt and pepper to taste
- 1 lb. spaghetti
- 7-8 basil leaves, chopped
- Pinch of oregano
- ¼ cup parsley
- Red pepper flakes(optional)

Directions: Sauté onion& garlic in oil using large sauté pan; low to medium heat. When onions are translucent, stir in anchovies and sauté until anchovies are dissolved.
Raise heat, add wine, bring to boil and stir in tomatoes, capers, olives, and red pepper flakes. Return to boil then lower heat and simmer five minutes. Season it with salt and pepper.

Cook spaghetti in rapidly boiling salted water until al dente. Just before serving, add basil and oregano to the sauce. Serve in individual dishes and sprinkle with fresh parsley.

 After draining spaghetti, return to pot with ½ cup sauce and ½ cup pasta water and toss to maintain moisture.

MANGIA BENE

PASTA AND BROCCOLI

Commentary: Think pasta primavera and add any other vegetable you prefer. For a burst of protein, add chicken pieces. For a bit of spice, I added sliced hot cherry peppers. Experiment, have fun and do it with love.

Ingredients: (serves four)

- 1 large head of broccoli (stems removed) or 1 bag of frozen florets
- 3 tablespoons of olive oil
- 1/2 cup of organic vegetable or chicken broth or water
- 3-5 cloves of garlic; sliced thinly
- salt and pepper to taste
- teaspoon of red pepper flakes (optional
- 1/2 cup of Kalamata olives; pitted and chopped
- 8 oz. of penne pasta or the pasta of your choice
- Grated cheese

Directions: Sauté the sliced garlic lightly in the olive oil using a large sauté pan that has a cover. Add the broccoli and ¼ cup of the broth. Steam it until it is almost fork tender. Add the Kalamata olives, salt and pepper, red pepper flakes and stir gently. Cook the penne, al dente, in salted water, drain, and reserve one cup of pasta water. Combine the pasta with the broccoli and serve. Add the remaining broth and/or pasta water to individual dishes to coat the mixture. Top with grated cheese. **Don't overcook the broccoli.**

MANGIA BENE

MINESTRONE

Commentary: My father made the best minestrone ever. I like it soupy, but others prefer a thick consistency. I never use tomatoes or tomato sauce, others do. It's a matter of taste. Either way it's a bean lover's delight filled with generous amounts of protein. Nothing is better on a cold winter's night along with some crusty Italian bread and red wine.

Ingredients:

- One 15 oz. can red kidney beans
- One 15 oz. can garbanzo beans
- One 15 oz. can cannellini beans
- 5-6 cloves chopped garlic
- ½ half large onion sliced thinly
- Salt & pepper to taste
- 1-2 cups string beans cut in half
- 1 cup of sliced red, green or yellow pepper
- One 32 oz. container of organic chicken broth
- 1/2 cup chopped celery
- ½ cup chopped carrots

- ¼ cup parsley
- Red pepper flakes(optional**)**
- 3 tablespoons olive oil

Directions:

Drain and rinse beans. Use a large heavy pot. Lightly sauté the onions, garlic, carrots, parsley, and celery in the olive oil. Add the beans, and cover the entire mixture with broth. You may need more broth during the cooking process to maintain enough liquid. Add salt and pepper to taste. Cover tightly and simmer for one hour.

MANGIA BENE

INSERT IMAGE #23

David Masliah and Karen Casale Masliah

ESCAROLE AND BEANS

Commentary: I love escarole but can't find any that is grown organically. I often substitute organic chard, kale or spinach instead of the escarole.

Ingredients:

- 1 large head of escarole thoroughly washed but not dried or rinsed; chopped into bite sized pieces
- 2 cans of cannellini beans; drained and rinsed
- 3-4 cloves of finely chopped garlic
- 2-3 tablespoons of olive oil
- Salt and pepper to taste
- 1 quart of Organic vegetable or chicken broth or water
- Grated cheese; parmigiana reggiano
- Red pepper flakes(optional)

Directions: Using a medium sized to large pot, sauté' the garlic in the olive oil over low to medium heat for one to two minutes without browning the garlic.

Add the wet chopped escarole, stir, cover tightly and steam the escarole until it completely wilts. Add the beans, cover the mixture with broth, salt and pepper to taste, cover the pot and simmer for 20 minutes.

Top with grated cheese. If you like a soupy mixture, add more broth. Soupy is best. Don't forget the crusty Italian bread.

MANGIA BENE

PASTINA

Commentary:
It doesn't get any simpler than this, and again, it wasn't fish. Pasta ruled. I ate it, loved it and still do. Here are two versions: my mother's version and my mother-in-law's version. Ida Colombo Fontanarosa was a talented cook. Both versions

used either elbow pasta, ditalini pasta or any small pasta. I'm sure you could use orzo.

Ingredients:

- Your choice of any small pasta (2-3 oz. per person)
- Butter
- One beaten egg(Ida's version)
- Grated cheese-optional
- Chopped parsley-optional
- Crushed red pepper-optional

Directions:

Carmel Puma Casale's version simply boiled the pasta of choice-about a half pound, drained it and added butter salt and pepper.

Ida Colombo Fontanrosa's version did basically the same thing but with less water. She added a beaten egg to the pasta when it was done. The four girls, Connie, Elaine, Ann and Janet ate it like soup. The egg added protein to this version. It sounds like Stracciatella, an Italian egg drop soup.
If desired, top it with your favorite grated cheese and parsley. I love it with crushed red pepper.

MANGIA BENE

EGGPLANT PARMAGIANA

Commentary: When I discovered the fried eggplant at Bella Napoli Italian Market in Juno Beach, FL, I never again bought a whole eggplant, peeled it and fried it. I buy them already fried. I use my father's incomparable sauce and fresh mozzarella and bake it in the oven until the cheese is melted. I get a lot of compliments; you will too.

When my father made this recipe, he peeled the eggplant, tried to slice it in even slices, salted each piece, put them in a colander, and placed a heavy cast iron frying pan on top of them to extract some of the moisture from the eggplants. Whew! I'm tired already. Of course, it was excellent.

Ingredients: (serves 4)

- 1 large eggplant
- 2 -3 eggs (whisked together)
- 2 c. breadcrumbs
- ½ c. olive oil
- ½ -1lb. mozzarella cheese (shredded or chunks)
- "The Sauce"

Directions:

Peel the eggplant and slice into ¼ inch slices. A mandolin works well for even slices. Follow the directions for veal parmigiana.
Note: The eggplant can be baked instead of fried. Don't worry about the moisture part.

INSERT IMAGE # 55

Part Five

Pasta e Pesce

Insert image #14

Commentary:

Before you begin this section, I must confess that I am a fish snob. I will not eat farm raised fish. I have never read anything positive about farmed raised fish which-according to my research- are fed artificially, swim around in their own waste, and attract parasites.

I eat only *wild* caught fish. I prefer locally caught fish and any cold water variety such as salmon and cod. Traders Joe's sells "frozen once" salmon. Some wild caught salmon, according to Trader Joe's are frozen, and sent to China for processing, fileting and then frozen again and sent back to the United States. Is there anything more critical than what you decide to consume as you strive for good health? I haven't researched this, but if China is touching my fish before it comes to my plate, I will not be happy.

I purchase all my fish from a local fish store/market that supplies many restaurants in my area.

AGLIO E OGLIO WITH CLAMS AND OR SHRIMP

pg. 55

Commentary: Follow my basic recipe for aglio e oglio and add clams, or shrimp or both. I have added crabmeat and lobster to this basic recipe. Enjoy, experiment, and do it with love.

Ingredients: (serves four)

- 5-8 large garlic cloves- sliced or chopped
- ½ cup fresh parsley-chopped fine(no stems)
- 2 anchovy filets
- 3-4 tablespoons of olive oil
- ¼ cup white wine
- ½ cup clam juice
- One can of diced clams with juice
- Large wild caught shrimp(enough for each person to have 5)
- ¾ lb. of linguini or spaghetti
- Grated cheese(optional)
- Red pepper flakes(optional)
- Salt and pepper

Directions:

Over low heat, sauté the anchovies until they melt. They will delicately flavor the mixture. Add the garlic and parsley and sauté in olive oil for two minutes. (DO NOT BROWN THE GARLIC UNLESS YOU WANT TO; I DON'T BUT SOME RESTAURANTS DO.

Add the clam juice and simmer slowly. Add the wine and let the mixture reduce. Add the clams and shrimp and cook until shrimp are pink on both sides. (5-7 minutes) Set aside until the pasta is done. **Do not overcook the clams and/or shrimp. They will lose their tenderness.**

Boil the pasta in salted water and cook until al-dente; save 2 ladles of the pasta water. Drain the pasta and add some of the pasta water to the mixture to keep it moist.

Place the pasta in individual dishes and ladle the clam and shrimp mixture over the pasta.

Spice it up with red pepper flakes and salt and pepper.

NOTE: Not all canned clams are created equal. Try different brands until you find the brand you like.

MANGIA BENE

SHRIMP MARINARA

Commentary: This is easy to make once you have mastered the king's sauce recipe. Marinara sauce cooks in about 30 minutes. This is one of the few times I add oregano to the sauce; pizza sauce is the other. Be careful with oregano; it's a powerful spice.

Ingredients: (serves four)

- 1 lb. wild caught shrimp-deveined(four to five large shrimp per person)
- 1 lb. spaghetti
- 1 teaspoon oregano
- ½ c. chopped parsley (fresh)
- Red pepper flakes-optional

- "The Sauce"-

Directions:

Boil four quarts of water in a large pot. Add salt to the boiling water and begin cooking the spaghetti. Cook "al dente" according to the directions. When the spaghetti is *almost* done place the shrimp in the simmering sauce and add the oregano. Stir until the shrimp are done (pink) then remove from heat. Drain the spaghetti, place it in individual dishes, and then ladle the sauce and shrimp over the individual portions. Top with parsley and serve. Add red pepper flakes if you want some spice.

MANGIA BENE

THE KING'S BASIC WHITE CLAM SAUCE

Commentary: My father's basic dislike for fish did not include clams. He made this regularly and we devoured it with any type of spaghetti. I prefer linguini which is how it is often served in restaurants.

Ingredients:

- One 15oz. can chopped clams/or use fresh clams
- One 8 oz. bottle clam juice
- 3-4 cloves garlic; finely chopped
- Salt and pepper to taste
- ½ c. white wine
- ¼ cup parsley; finely chopped
- 1 tsp. oregano

- Red pepper flakes(optional)

Directions:

Gently sauté the garlic and parsley for 2-3 minutes on low to medium heat. Add the canned clams and the juice that is in the can. Add salt, pepper, oregano and some of the clam juice. A soupy consistency is best. Simmer for two minutes then add the wine. Simmer for two more minutes; do not boil. Serve over spaghetti or linguini.

Note: Canned clams or fresh clams cook very quickly. Do not overcook the clams or they will be too chewy. Find a tender variety that you like. Seawatch is the best but I can't find them. Try on-line. The boiled variety is also excellent.

MANGIA BENE

Shrimp Scampi

Commentary: (Serves 4)
I love shrimp and usually just add it to my clam sauce recipe or marinara recipe and serve it over linguini. I have ordered several versions of Scampi at restaurants and it always seemed to be served differently. It has more ingredients than I am used to using, but it is worth the outcome. Most of these ingredients are staples.

Ingredients:
- 16-18 wild caught large raw shrimp-peeled and deveined
- ¼ cup olive oil
- ¼ cup unsalted butter
- ¼ cup white wine
- 4-6 cloves of finely chopped garlic
- 2 tablespoons fresh finely chopped parsley
- 1 tsp. lemon zest

Page 59

- Salt and pepper to taste
- Crushed red pepper-optional

Directions:

Use a deep sided frying pan. Lightly sauté' the garlic & parsley for 1-2 minutes in the olive oil over medium heat. (Don't brown the garlic; don't leave the stove) Add the butter and heat until bubbly. Add the white wine and lemon zest and reduce to half.
Add the shrimp and cook until pink turning them on both sides.
Add salt and pepper and crushed pepper if desired.
Serve over rice, couscous, or orzo and top with fresh parsley.

Insert image #16
The Blessed Siblings
Fran, Jimmy, Stephanie, Joe

Part Six

Sunday Pasta

INSERT IMAGE # 12

LASAGNA

Commentary: Who doesn't love lasagna? I never order it in a restaurant because my father made the best and spoiled me forever. Remember, it's the sauce that makes these dishes special. When my friends invite me for dinner and cook Italian, I always compliment them. I hope I sound sincere.

Ingredients:

- 1lb. box of lasagna
- 1lb. ricotta cheese
- 1lb. mozzarella cheese (grated)
- 2 eggs
- ½ c. parsley(finely chopped)
- 1teaspoon salt
- 1teaspoon pepper
- Grated cheese
- "The Sauce"

Directions:

In a large bowl combine the ricotta, mozzarella, eggs, parsley and salt and pepper. Mix with a fork until all ingredients are evenly distributed. Boil lasagna until it is "al dente". Drain lasagna, pat each piece dry and set aside on top of paper towels or a clean dish towel.

Use a 2-3 inch deep baking dish and cover the bottom with some sauce. Spread out a layer of lasagna with sides touching but not overlapping. Spread a layer of the cheese mixture evenly over the lasagna and top with some sauce. Repeat until you are at the top of the dish. Top layer must be only lasagna and some sauce. Bake at 325 for one hour. Remove from oven and let stand for 15 minutes. Serve with more sauce, grated cheese and the king's meatballs, sausage or both.

Note: If lasagna pasta sections are longer than your pan, cut them to fit.

MANGIA BENE

BAKED MANICOTTI

Commentary: Manicotti is a popular dish and easy to prepare when you purchase the frozen variety. The *sauce* is the difference maker. It's always a winner.

Ingredients: (serves four)

- 1 lb. Manicotti(frozen or fresh from the store)
- ½ cup chopped basil (optional)
- Grated cheese (optional)
- "The Sauce"

Directions:

Purchase the manicotti at an Italian specialty store or your favorite supermarket. It is usually frozen. Ladle some sauce on the bottom of a baking dish and some on top. Cover tightly, and bake according to directions on the package. When finished, sprinkle chopped basil on top and serve. It's all about the sauce. Serve with your favorite Italian meat: meatballs, sausage, and or braciola.

MANGIA BENE

BAKED ZITI

Commentary: This is easier to prepare than lasagna. If you having a big crowd, it's ideal. Always use fresh ingredients and buy your cheese the same day or a day before. Check the dates, especially for the ricotta.

Ingredients: (serves four)

- 1 lb. Ziti
- 1lb. ricotta
- 1lb. shredded mozzarella
- 2 eggs
- ½c. Chopped parsley
- 1 teaspoon each salt & pepper
- Grated cheese (parmigiana reggiano)
- "The Sauce"

Directions:

. Combine the same ingredients as in the lasagna recipe. Mix thoroughly. When ziti is done-al dente- combine it with the cheese mixture so all ingredients are evenly distributed. Cover the bottom of the baking dish with sauce and fill the dish or pan with the entire mixture. Ladle some sauce on top and cover tightly. Bake at 350 until the cheese is melted and it is heated through. This should take about 40 minutes.

Serve with grated cheese and your favorite meat.

BUON APPETITO

BAKED RAVIOLI

Commentary: That's right, baked ravioli .I love how easy this is to prepare. You don't have to boil the ravioli, or strain it and worry about too much water infiltrating your sauce. Buy it fresh or frozen, layer it like you would lasagna, and bake it. Thirty minutes at 325 and it's done and ready to serve. When the sauce is already prepared, this dish is a cinch.

Ingredients:

- I bag/box of fresh or frozen ravioli
- "the sauce"
- Fresh basil or parsley for garnish

Directions:

Layer the bottom of the pan with some sauce and layer the ravioli. Place a thin amount of sauce between each layer and on top. Cover tightly with foil and bake at 325 for 30 minutes.

Mangia Bene

SIMPLE BOLOGNESE

Commentary:

This was not something we ate in the Casale household. I believe this sauce has its roots in Northern Italy. I do not, until September 2014, ever remember consuming a pasta dish with a Bolognese sauce. Why now Jimmy? I'm glad you asked.

My dear friend and fellow Marine, Billy Cook, loves this sauce, orders it all the time in restaurants, and thoroughly enjoys his wife's version which she makes in large batches so it can be frozen and eaten again and again. Diane, Billy's wife, makes a delicious, but more complicated recipe which includes not only ground beef but ground pork and ground veal. Billy loves it.

I decided to surprise Billy at a family dinner (Diane was not there) by making the Casale interpretation of this sauce. Billy loved it which inspired me to include it in the revised version of the Casale Family Cookbook and Memories.

Ingredients: (serves 6)

- Start with the classic marinara sauce recipe.
- 1 lb. of ground beef (I have been using grass fed beef. It has a superior flavor and texture)
- 1 lb. ground Italian sausage-hot or sweet or both

Directions:

Sauté the ground beef and ground sausage in a large frying pan until it is brown and crumbly (no big pieces). Drain off the fat. Add the meat to the sauce and simmer for 45-60 minutes.(This does not make it gravy)

Notes:

As always, adjust or adapt this to your liking. I call this my lazy sauce because I do not have to make meatballs or fry sausage. It's so simple. So far, it has been a big hit with family and friends. Freeze the leftover sauce and enjoy again and again. I have also made it with ground sausage. I use hot and sweet sausage (two of each) and fry it separately from the ground beef. Sausage adds even more flavor.
Do it all with love and enjoy.

MANGIA BENE

VODKA SAUCE

Commentary: I don't remember my father or mother ever making this sauce. The first time I experienced this sauce was in a restaurant in

Eastchester, called *Ciao*. I think it was in the 1980s. I loved it but never considered making my own version until this year.

Ingredients:

- Your basic marinara sauce plus:
- 3-4 shallots
- ½ cup vodka
- 2/3 cup of half and half or heavy cream
- ½ cup Grated cheese
- Fresh basil

Directions:

Make your basic marinara sauce but sauté the shallots first. Add the garlic and parsley when the shallots are tender. Don't brown the garlic.

When the sauce is simmering, add the vodka and allow it to cook off for about seven minutes. Stir in the cream which **must be room temperature. Hint:** Microwave the cream for 10 to 15 seconds. Test it its warmness with your finger. Three minutes later, add the cheese and fresh basil. Cook for about 30 minutes. **Note:** Some recipes call for peas and pieces of ham.

MANGIA BENE

Part Seven

This n' That

INSERT IMAGE #21

Caprese Salad

Commentary: This is the quintessential Italian hors d' oeuvre served in most Italian restaurants before dinner. The ingredients are basically the same everywhere, but, as always, the freshest ingredients make a difference. I usually like to drizzle a little olive oil over the finished product, but now I am adding vinaigrette that includes chopped capers and red wine vinegar (consider this optional if you don't like capers).

Ingredients:

- Vine ripe organic tomotatoes-1/4 inch thick slices
- Fresh mozzarella cheese -1/4 inch thick slices
- First pressed extra virgin olive oil
- Salt and freshly ground pepper
- 2 Tsps. finely chopped capers
- Red wine vinegar
- Fresh basil leaves(large**)**

Directions:

Layer the mozzarella, tomatoes, and basil leaves as follows: cheese slices first on the bottom; next layer the large basil leaves; place the tomatoes on top of basil leaves. Now lightly salt and pepper this beautiful presentation which represents the three colors of the Italian flag.

Whisk together the olive oil, vinegar and capers and drizzle over the Caprese Salad.

Antipasto

Commentary: There are so many ways to serve this Italian specialty. This is an opportunity to make it your own because you are free to use your favorite Italian cold cuts, cheeses and other delicacies. My father taught me to make it with love. He loved people, he loved entertaining and he loved the look on his guests' faces as they happily consumed his savory dishes. Focus on the presentation. Your guests will *not* be disappointed.

Ingredients:
- **Cold cuts**(choose at least two or three of your favorites thinly sliced)
- ¼ lb.Genoa salami
- ¼ lb.Capicola
- ¼ lb.Pepperoni
- ¼ lb.Ham
- ¼ lb.Soppressata
- ¼ lb. prizzute
- **Cheeses**
- ¼ lb. Provolone(thinly sliced or the aged provolone cut into chunks)
- ¼ lb.Mozzarella, regular or smoked,(I use thick slices)
- **Other delicacies**(choose at least two)
- Roasted peppers cut into thin strips
- Olives of your choice
- Pepperoncini
- Artichoke hearts
- **Basics**
- Lettuce leaves
- Italian bread(thinly sliced)
- Vinaigrette or olive oil

Directions:
Layer the large lettuce leaves on the bottom of your favorite platter. The size of the platter is dictated by the number of guests.
Roll each piece of meat and cheese into shapes that resemble a little cigar.

Place the meat and cheeses on the edge of the platter and alternate them for a striking variation in color

Place thin strips of red roasted pepper in between every second or third slice of meat and cheese.-Place olives and artichoke hearts in the center of the platter. Lightly drizzle with your Italian vinaigrette.

Insert image #20

MANGIA BENE

MUFFULETTA: The Round Wedge

Commentary:

As far as I'm concerned, there is no such thing as an Italian sub or hero or -God forbid- a hoagie. Yes, you can have a salami or bologna sandwich, but if you put several types of Italian cold cuts and chesses on a loaf of Italian bread, you have my permission to call it a *wedge*.

We Harrisonites and 50s rock n rollers referred to the use of any cold cut placed inside Cassone's loaf of Italian bread as a *wedge*. That's right, a wedge was any length-sometimes the whole loaf-of Italian bread cut in half and filled with your favorite sliced meats and cheeses and assorted toppings like lettuce, tomatoes, peppers etc. This also includes meatballs and sausage.

Back in ancient times there was a place in Mamaroneck, NY on the Post Road called the *Wedge King*. Though we made our own wedges most of the time, we occasionally went to this establishment. The conversation went something like this:

Man behind the counter, "Whatdaya want kid?" Me, "Gimme a sausage and peppers wedge."

And if sausage and peppers were not your thing, you could have your Italian bread packed with any of the following: meatballs, sausage, eggplant, steak and, of course, your favorite meats and cheeses: salami, bologna, capicola, ham, mortadella, prizzute, olive loaf, provolone, mozzarella, peppers and eggs and more. I knew a kid from Port Chester, NY who was a caddie at the Harrison Country Club. He put spaghetti in his wedge. I love spaghetti; but that's over the line.

These memories are making me hungry so let's get back to The Muffaletta, a delicious and delectable concoction that will impress your friends and satisfy your inner yearnings for something Italian.

Ingredients:
- 1 round loaf of Italian bread. The kind with a whole in the middle. If you can't find it at an Italian bakery, move to an Italian neighborhood.
- ¼ lb. each of your favorite cold cuts(slice thinly)
- ½ red onion slice thinly
- ¼ pound each of provolone and mozzarella(sliced thinly)
- Enough arugula to go around the loaf
- Enough chopped roasted peppers to go around the loaf
- Enough chopped black olives to go around the loaf
- Drizzle your vinaigrette on both sides of the bread *before* you start loading it up with the ingredients

Basic Vinaigrette

- 2-3 clove of finely chopped garlic
- 1 tsp. oregano
- 2 oz. light olive oil-whisk in slowly after combining the other ingredients
- ¼ cup red wine vinegar
- Freshly ground pepper

Directions:
Cut the loaf in half and hollow out both sides.-Drizzle each half with vinaigrette. Layer the bottom with your meats and cheeses.-Top with onion slices, olives, peppers and arugula. Cut into WEDGES and serve. As always, do it your way.

MANGIA BENE

STUFFED ARTICHOKES

Commentary: My mother's artichokes have precipitated a few arguments between me and a few servers in Italian restaurants. When I specifically asked if the artichokes were stuffed, I was told they were. But when they came out with some ridiculous dipping sauce, a less than civil conversation began about what is a real stuffed artichoke. I learned my lesson after two tries; I no longer order them unless I know my mother or my sister Stephanie are in the kitchen.

Ingredients:

- Six medium sized artichokes
- 3 cups breadcrumbs

- ¾ cup chopped parsley
- 4-5 cloves finely chopped garlic
- 3 cups grated cheese
- Salt & pepper to taste
- Olive oil as needed

Directions:

Cut the stems so artichokes will sit flat in a large pot. Using a scissor, trim the sharp leaves at the top of each artichoke, then pound the top with your hand which allow leaves to spread open at the top. Combine all ingredients except the olive oil and stuff the mixture between the leaves pushing mixture to the bottom of each leaf. Next, drizzle some olive oil into each of the stuffed leaves. Add water to the pot only up to the bottom of the artichoke. Cover and simmer until the leaves can be removed easily. You may have to add water periodically due to evaporation. Total time could be one to two hours. Keep checking for doneness.

MANGIA BENE

MANGIA BENE

NAAN PIZZA

Commentary: My daughter Karen is a great cook. She loves to try new things and experiment with variations of recipes. Her easy Naan pizza is quick and delicious and eliminates buying and preparing dough. Your home made pizza sauce is your basic marinara sauce with the addition of oregano. Vary your ingredients and have fun with this recipe.

Ingredients:

- One Naan bread from the supermarket
- The Sauce; add a tsp. of oregano to your marinara sauce
- One 8 oz. package of shredded whole milk mozzarella
- ½ red onion; thinly sliced
- Fresh spinach; julienned (enough to cover top)

- ¼ cup crumbled blue cheese

Directions:

Spread sauce evenly over the Naan bread. Next spread the mozzarella cheese over the sauce. Top off with onion, spinach and blue cheese and place in a 400 degree oven for 10 – 12 minutes until the mozzarella is bubbling. Experiment with your favorite toppings.

MANGIA BENE

CHOCOLATE DIPPED ORANGE BISCOTTI

Commentary: Karen also bakes. Her DNA, though half Scottish, is classic Casale and Puma. She inherited our addiction to sweets. Biscotti-if you're Italian is designed to dunk in your coffee.

Ingredients:

- I cup all-purpose flour
- 1/2 cup sugar
- ¼ teaspoon baking powder
- ¼ teaspoon baking soda
- ¼ teaspoon salt
- 1 egg
- 1 egg white
- ½ cup chopped almonds
- 2 tablespoons of orange zest

- 4 one oz. squares bittersweet chocolate

Directions:

Preheat oven to 350 degrees. Grease a cookie sheet. Stir together the flour, sugar, baking soda, baking powder and salt. Beat egg and egg white then mix in almonds and zest. Knead dough by hand and form into a smooth ball. Form the dough into a log shape about 10 inches long and 6 inches wide. Bake 25 minutes then let cool on a rack. Using a serrated knife cut one inch slices, place slices on their side, place slices back on cookie sheet, and bake an additional 20-25 minutes. Turn over half way through the baking process. Melt the chocolate using a double boiler or the microwave. Allow chocolate to cool but not harden before dipping one side of the biscotti into the chocolate. Place cookies onto wire racks until cool and dry.

MANGIA BENE

TIRAMASU TRIFLE PIE

Commentary: I never met anyone who didn't like Tiramisu. Karen's version is quick and easy. Enjoy.

Ingredients:

- 1&1/2 tablespoons instant coffee granules
- ¾ cup warm water

- One 10-11 oz. frozen pound cake
- One 8oz. container mascarpone cheese
- ½ cup powdered sugar
- ½ cup chocolate syrup
- One 12 oz. container frozen whipped topping; thawed
- 2 English toffee candy bars; coarsely chopped

Direction:

Stir coffee into warm water to dissolve and let cool. Cut pound cake into 14 slices then cut again diagonally. Place the triangle slices into a 9" cake pan along the bottom and sides. Drizzle coffee mixture over cake. Use an electric mixer to mix the cheese, sugar and syrup. Add half of the whipped topping and mix again until light and fluffy. Spread the mixture evenly over the cake and top with the remaining whipped cream. Chill eight hours.

Insert image #42

David, Olivia, Karen, Luca, Meemaw(Cathy Bisland Casale)

Part Eight

Family Pictures

Insert images #s
24,25,26,31,36,37,38,39,48,32,54,51

pg. 79

Made in the USA
Columbia, SC
27 December 2019